Drawing Fun Fashions

ROCK STAR
Style

FUN FASHIONS YOU CAN SKETCH

By **Mari Bolte**   illustrated by **Sarah Dahl**

Snap books®

CAPSTONE PRESS
a capstone imprint

Table of Contents

Getting Started

Each outfit shows step-by-step instructions on how to draw your very own fashion model. Build upon simple shapes, and use erasable guidelines to create a human shape.

STEP 1: Start with a simple line drawing. Pick your favorite pose, and use light guidelines to build your model.

TIP: Want to try digital art? There are many free or inexpensive drawing and painting apps available for tablets and smartphones.

STEP 2: Darken the outlines, and start adding in details like hemlines and hand placements.

STEP 3: Erase guidelines, and draw in things such as fabric prints, hair, facial features, and accessories.

STEP 4: Finish any final details and then add in color, textures, and shading to bring your model to life.

TIP: Go beyond crayons and markers. Try pastels, watercolor paints or pencils, and charcoal to find a style that works for you.

POWER BALLAD

Animal print and ripped denim have been fashion picks for rock stars of any era. Rock the ages with these timeless threads.

TIP: Use whites and very light blues to recreate distressed denim.

SCHOOL OF ROCK

Dress for success at the school of hard knocks. Bring some rock star flair to the boring world of suits and ties. Red accents bring this outfit to a whole new level.

TIP: When it comes to red, a little can go a long way. Use it to enhance the outfit's colors without letting it take over.

Little Miss METALHEAD

Steal the show with big splashes of color. Accessories are what makes this outfit pop. Belts, bangles, and boots hold everything together.

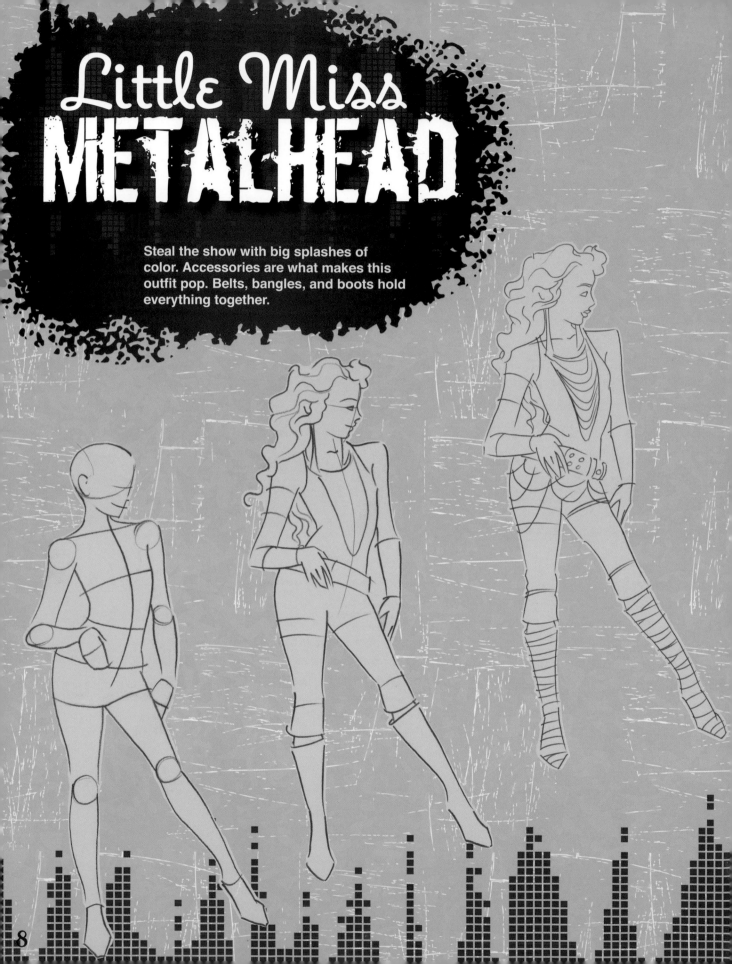

TIP: Metallic tones help the accessories in this outfit stand out. Try using metallic paint instead of regular pens for a look that shines.

LET'S SHRED

Rock stars have to look good any time, any where. Paparazzi could be waiting around any corner! Take style over the edge with a shredded dress and spikes to match.

TIP: Pale colors look great with metallic accents. Instead of silver, try copper, gold, or gunmetal gray.

CROSSOVER ARTIST

Launch the rock star wardrobe to new levels with a fresh look. Keep rocker cred with military-inspired style and bright colors. Plaids lend a touch of everyday fashion to the look.

TIP: Glow-in-the-dark paint will add an extreme effect to the boots and shirt.

FUSION FASHION

Put the party into party rock! A ruffled skirt and a chic bag are all you need to stand out. The world spins around you when you look like a star.

TIP: A fine-tip pen adds a new level of detail to this outfit.

OUTFIT OF THE YEAR

Dazzle the room with an outfit that's truly worthy of a rock star. Be bold by picking patterns that both clash and contrast.

TIP: Reproduce the spattered look of the boots with paint. Lightly flick a paintbrush loaded with acrylic or watercolor paint over plain black boots.

ROCK ROYALTY

Some become stars by twists of
fate. Others are born famous. Rock
royalty dresses like there's a concert
happening every night.

TIP: Give the jacket
a real leather look by
using soft matte colors.

HARD ROCK RIFFS

Storm the stage with star power! Zippers, spikes, and metal feel feminine with the addition of purple and bright green. Sing your heart out and shout your style out loud.

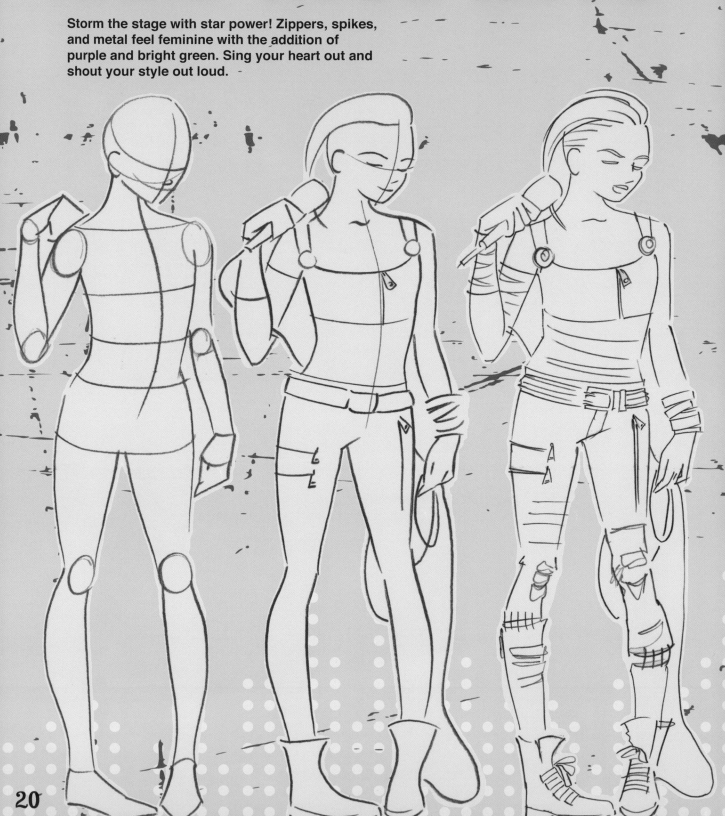

TIP: Colored pencils, pastel pencils, or thin-tipped permanent markers will help the plaid pants pop.

SOFT METAL

Not all rock stars love studs and metal. Some stars have a softer shine! Add some truly girly flair with a ruffled skirt and a lace top.

TIP: Watercolor pencils will give you the soft, flowy look of the skirt. Use them lightly to copy the pattern on the lace shirt too.

COVER
ARTIST

Choosing a great outfit is as important to a rock star as picking a great song. Killer accessories ensure this collection is more than a one-hit wonder.

TIP: Go wild with patterns! If plain pants aren't your thing, experiment with animal prints, bold stripes, or bright graphics.

Country Solo

Go back to the country with classic
cowgirl style. Linen, leather, and country
girl sass guarantee an outfit straight from
Nashville's Music Row.

TIP: For extra impact, use a silver pen to add small studs to the jacket. Or add swirly lines to the boots with a turquoise marker.

PARTY IN THE DARK

Light up the night in a neon-inspired gown. The bright rings will guarantee that this rock star's glow doesn't go out.

TIP: Use scratchboard with rainbow colors underneath for a realistic effect. Etch the design onto the scratchboard. The rainbow colors will make up the lines of the dress.

Extra Accessories

Use your creativity to create original accessories for each outfit. Each piece will reflect your personal style and taste! Take your time and figure out what works for you. Don't forget that accessories complete the outfit.

TIP: Glam, grunge, indie, new wave, punk, metal, pop, goth. These are all inspiring words for the rock star's wardrobe!

TIP: Explore fashion trends starting in the 1950s through today. Many styles have stayed popular throughout the years. Others have fallen out of fashion only to return in later eras.

Read More

Hibbert, Claire. *Pop Star.* Celeb.
Mankato, Minn.: Sea-to-Sea
Publications, 2012.

Thomas, Isabel. *Being a Fashion Stylist.*
Awesome Jobs. Minneapolis: Lerner
Publications Co., 2013.

Wilson, Rosie. *Fashion Industry.*
A Closer Look: Global Industries.
New York: Rosen Central, 2011.

Internet Sites

FactHound offers a safe, fun way to find Internet
sites related to this book. All of the sites on
FactHound have been researched by our staff.

Here's all you do:

Visit *www.facthound.com*

Type in this code: 9781620650363

Super-cool stuff! Check out projects, games and lots more at
www.capstonekids.com

Snap Books are published by Capstone Press,
1710 Roe Crest Drive, North Mankato, Minnesota 56003
www.capstonepub.com

Library of Congress Cataloging-in-Publication Data
Bolte, Mari.
  Rock star style : fun fashions you can sketch / by Mari Bolte.
     pages cm. — (Snap. Drawing fun fashions)
  Summary: "Lively text and fun illustrations describe how to draw cool fashions"—Provided by publisher.
  ISBN 978-1-62065-036-3 (library binding)
  ISBN 978-1-4765-1785-8 (ebook PDF)

1. Fashion drawing—Juvenile literature. 2. Rock musicians—Clothing—Juvenile literature. I. Title.

TT509.B654 2013
741.6'72—dc23   2012028400

Editorial Credits
Lori Bye, designer; Nathan Gassman, art director; Marcie Spence, media researcher;
    Laura Manthe, production specialist

The illustrations in this book were created digitally.
Design elements by Shutterstock.

Printed in the United States of America in North Mankato, Minnesota.
092012   006933CGS13